time to
EAT

Written and Illustrated by

Steve Jenkins and Robin Page

Houghton Mifflin Books for Children • Houghton Mifflin Harcourt • Boston New York 2011

What's your favorite food? It's probably not worms, blood, or elephant droppings, but there are animals that thrive on these foods.

And it's not just what animals eat that can be unusual. Many animals have surprising ways of collecting, storing, and consuming their food. They may wrap it in silk, roll it in a ball, or glue it to their skin. There are animals that eat the same food at every meal, others that gulp down just about anything, and a few that take a little taste first, just to make sure they like what's for dinner.

The **giant panda** chews on bamboo shoots for twelve hours a day.

Not shoots and leaves again!

6,000 milk shakes

The **tick** feeds on just one thing: the blood of a living animal. It may wait years for a meal, but when the tick finally does eat, it can consume as much as one hundred times its own weight in blood. You'd have to slurp down about 6,000 milk shakes to have a meal of equivalent size.

Live worms — for

The **shrew** needs a lot of energy to keep its tiny body warm. If it goes more than two or three hours without eating, it can die of starvation.

breakfast, lunch, and dinner

I just hope I can remember where I put it.

The **acorn woodpecker** chisels a hole in a tree trunk, then wedges an acorn in place. Acorn woodpeckers can tuck as many as 50,000 acorns into a single tree.

Funny face

The **chipmunk's** cheek
pouches stretch to hold
an astounding number
of nuts and seeds. The
chipmunk stores this food
in its burrow to snack
on later.

A **butcherbird** grabs an unlucky grasshopper and impales it on a sharp thorn. This holds the insect in place while the bird eats it, or keeps it handy for a future meal.

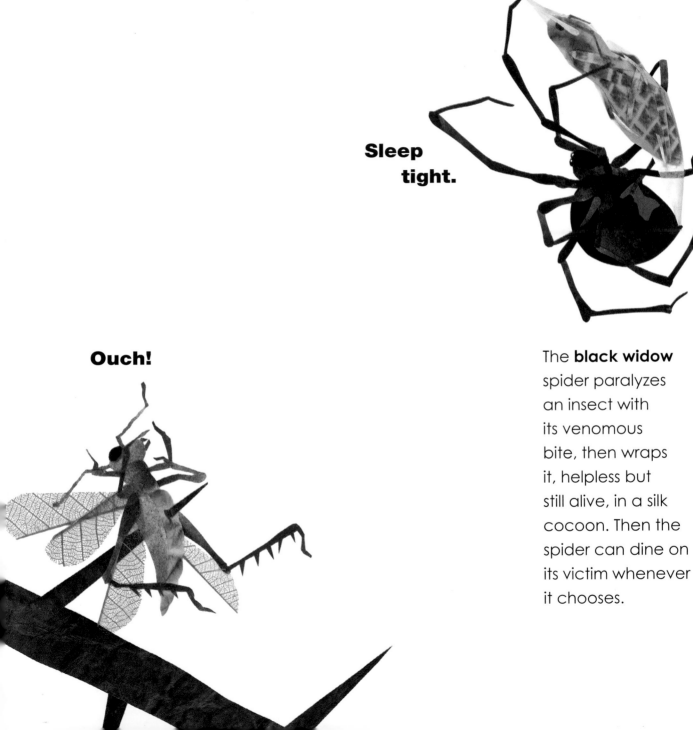

Sleep tight.

Ouch!

The **black widow** spider paralyzes an insect with its venomous bite, then wraps it, helpless but still alive, in a silk cocoon. Then the spider can dine on its victim whenever it chooses.

Crunchy, chewy, and inside out

The sticky, mucus-covered skin of the **crucifix toad** makes a convenient place to store captured insects. The toad regularly sheds its skin — pulling it off over its head the way you take off a sweater — then eats it, bugs and all.

I can't believe I ate the whole thing!

The **anaconda** swallows its prey whole. It can gulp down an animal as large as a deer or pig, and has even been known to devour a jaguar. The anaconda needs only four or five meals a year.

Plants make up most of the **ostrich's** diet. This bird has no teeth, however, so it can't chew its food. Instead, it swallows rocks, which are stored in a chamber next to its stomach. The rocks help grind up the leaves and grass that the ostrich eats.

Rock candy

The **dung beetle** eats animal dung — poop. The beetle shapes the dung into a ball, then rolls it to its underground home. There, the dung ball will provide food for the beetle, its mate, and their offspring.

It's a dirty job . . .

This baby **pelican** is too young to hunt on its own. Instead, it reaches deep into its mother's throat and enjoys a meal of regurgitated fish.

Just a little farther . . .

With a mouth shaped like a long, narrow tube, the **giant hawk moth** drinks nectar from a rare orchid. No other creature can sip the sweet liquid deep inside this flower.

The **aye-aye** taps on dead trees, rousing beetles and other creatures that live beneath the bark. When it detects movement, the aye-aye chews into the wood and snags its prey with a long, thin middle finger.

Knock, knock!

It might prefer to eat fish, but the **tiger shark** will swallow just about anything. Shoes, license plates, bottles, and even pieces of rubber tires have been found in the stomach of this shark.

Garbage disposal

The **black rat** also eats a wide variety of foods, but it is more cautious than a shark. To make sure a new food isn't dangerous, one rat in a pack will take a nibble and wait a little while. If it doesn't get sick, the rat and its companions will eat more.

You first!

Got milk?

Like all mammals, the baby
blue whale drinks milk. A *lot* of
milk — the equivalent of 800
glasses every day. On this rich
diet, a young whale can gain
200 pounds (91 kilograms)
every twenty-four hours.

**What would
you like
for *your*
next meal?**

To learn more
about the animals
in this book, turn
the page.

The **giant panda** lives in the mountains of China. Humans have destroyed much of the panda's forest habitat and the bamboo groves that provide its food, and only about 1,600 of these bears are left in the wild. Pandas may appear cute and cuddly, but they are large animals and can be dangerous if they feel threatened. A male giant panda can weigh as much as 250 pounds (113 kilograms). Females are a little smaller.

The **common wood tick,** which is about ⅛ inch (3 millimeters) long, is found in wooded and brushy habitats throughout the world. A tick will cling to a twig or blade of grass and wait — sometimes for years — for a passing animal to brush against it. The tick then climbs aboard, attaches itself with sharp jaws, and sucks its host's blood. Ticks often carry diseases, and their bite can be dangerous to humans.

The **northern short-tailed shrew** lives in forests and meadows in the northeastern United States. It's about five inches (12½ centimeters) long, including its tail. Shrews are small, fierce predators. A shrew can consume three times its own body weight every day, eating insects, worms, snails, and small animals. It will even kill and eat other shrews.

Acorn woodpeckers are common in open woodlands in the western United States and Mexico. This bird reaches nine inches (23 centimeters) in length, and feeds on insects, fruit, and nuts. It gets its name from its practice of storing acorns in tree trunks, buildings, fences, and even automobile grills.

Chipmunks are most common in North America, but they also live in Asia and eastern Europe. These rodents are about six inches (15 centimeters) long. They dig underground burrows or make their homes in hollow logs or piles of rocks. Chipmunks feed on seeds, nuts, and berries as well as insects and birds' eggs. They store much of their food, carrying it to their nests in expandable cheek pouches.

The **butcherbird,** or shrike, gets its name from its practice of impaling its prey — insects or small animals — on a thorn or sharp tree branch. There are many different kinds of shrike, found throughout much of the world. The gray-headed bush shrike — the bird shown in this book — is about 14 inches (36 centimeters) long and lives in wooded areas in southern Africa.

The most venomous spider in North America is the female **black widow** spider. Its bite is painful but rarely fatal to humans. Including her legs, the female black widow measures about 1½ inches (4 centimeters) across. Males, which are much smaller, are not poisonous. Black widows can be identified by a red hourglass-shaped mark on their bellies. They prefer to spin their disorderly webs in dark, sheltered places. Black widows are found in temperate climates around the world. They eat insects, other spiders, and even small reptiles and mammals. Sometimes a female black widow eats her mate — a habit that has given this spider its name.

The **crucifix toad,** also known as the holy cross toad, gets its name from a cross-shaped mark on its back. It lives in dry regions of Australia. During a drought, the toad buries itself underground and doesn't emerge until it rains. The sticky glue that coats this toad's skin may be a foul-tasting protection against predators as well as a way to store food. Crucifix toads are small amphibians, only about 2½ inches (6 centimeters) in length. They eat ants, termites, and other insects.

The **anaconda** lives in South American rainforests, where it spends most of its time in lakes and rivers. The longest anaconda ever captured measured 30 feet (9 meters) long. The reticulated python of Southeast Asia can be longer, but the anaconda is easily the heaviest snake in the world, tipping the scales at up to 550 pounds (250 kilograms). It is a constrictor, a snake that kills not with poison but with its powerful coils, wrapping them around its prey and squeezing until its victim can't breathe. The anaconda's teeth are designed for grabbing prey, not chewing, so the animals they catch — birds, small mammals, alligators, and even pigs and deer — are swallowed whole.

The **ostrich**, which can reach nine feet in height (274 grams) and weigh 350 pounds (159 kilograms), is the largest bird on earth. It is much too big to fly, but it is a fast runner and can outrace a horse. Ostriches live on the plains of Africa, where they feed on leaves, seeds, fruit, insects, and the occasional frog or small mammal. An ostrich may carry more than two pounds (1 kilogram) of stones in its gizzard, a muscular pouch that is part of the digestive system. Food passing through the gizzard on its way to the stomach is ground up by the stones, making it easier to digest.

Dung beetles live on every continent except Antarctica. There are thousands of different species of dung beetle, but they all eat animal droppings. Without these beetles, habitats with many grazing animals, such as the African savannah, would become almost completely covered in animal waste. Burying the droppings helps fertilize new plants and reduce pests, such as flies, that live in animal waste. Dung beetles range in size from insects almost too small to see to 2½-inch- (6-centimeter-) long giants. Dung beetles that make balls are called rollers, and they can maneuver balls that weigh fifty times as much as they do. Other dung beetles are known as tunnelers. They burrow directly beneath a pile of droppings, and the dung drops into their tunnel. A third kind of beetle, the dwellers, move into a pile of animal droppings and eat it from the inside out.

Pelicans live along warm seacoasts in most parts of the world. They are large birds, with wingspans of more than ten feet (3 meters). Pelicans are known for their elastic throat pouch. Several birds often glide in a line just above the water, diving in when they spot fish near the surface. When a pelican hits the water, its throat pouch expands, fills with water, and, if the bird is lucky, holds a fish or two. The pelican strains the water out of its bill and gulps down the fish.

At 14 inches (36 centimeters) in length, the tongue of **the giant hawk moth** is the longest in the insect world. The moth itself is huge, with a wingspan of more than twelve inches (30 centimeters). It lives in Madagascar and southern Africa, and feeds on the nectar of a rare orchid. The nectar lies at the bottom of a tube, or spur, that is over a foot long. As the moth feeds, it carries pollen from flower to flower. In 1862, the naturalist Charles Darwin predicted that an insect with an extremely long tongue must exist to pollinate this orchid. More than forty years later, the giant hawk moth was discovered.

The **aye-aye** is a tree-dwelling primate found only in the rainforests of Madagascar. Its body is about 16 inches (41 centimeters) long, with a bushy tail that is longer than its body. In addition to insects, it feeds on fruit, nectar, and birds' eggs. The aye-aye is active at night, and like many nocturnal animals it has large eyes. These eyes, along with its pointed ears and sharp claws, give this gentle animal a somewhat frightening appearance. Native people consider it an omen of bad luck and often kill it on sight. For this reason, and because its rainforest home is being destroyed to make room for farms and towns, the aye-aye is seriously endangered.

The **tiger shark** is a large and very dangerous predator — only the great white shark is responsible for more attacks on humans. This shark cruises warm coastal seas throughout the world and gets its name from the dark vertical stripes on its sides. It can reach 16 feet (5 meters) in length and weigh as much as a small car. These sharks are famous for eating almost anything, but most of their diet consists of fish, birds, seals, and turtles.

The **black rat**, also known as the ship rat, originated in Asia. Over the centuries it has traveled with humans to towns and cities throughout the world, but it is most common in warm, coastal climates. Black rats are serious pests, eating and soiling grain and other stored food. Rats may also carry dangerous diseases, including bubonic plague — the infamous Black Death of the Middle Ages. Black rats have a body about eight inches (20 centimeters) long, with a tail that is about the same length.

As far as we know, the **blue whale** is the largest animal that has ever lived. It grows to more than 100 feet (30 meters) in length. The record weight for a blue whale is 390,000 pounds (177,000 kilograms) — more than 5,000 typical eleven-year-old children. A newborn blue whale weighs about 5,500 pounds (2,500 kilograms). Blue whales are found throughout the world's oceans, though it is estimated that there are no more than 12,000 left — a small fraction of the number that existed before commercial whaling began. The blue whale is a filter feeder. It swims through dense swarms of shrimplike animals called krill, gulping in huge mouthfuls of seawater. Then, with a tongue the size of a station wagon, the whale forces the water through a set of bony plates — called baleen — that line its mouth. The krill is left behind and swallowed. One blue whale can eat millions of krill in a day.

For Alec — S.J. & R.P.

Houghton Mifflin Books for Children is an imprint of Houghton Mifflin Harcourt Publishing Company.

www.hmhbooks.com

The text of this book is set in Century Gothic.
The illustrations are torn- and cut-paper collage.

Library of Congress Cataloging-in-Publication Data

Jenkins, Steve, 1952–
   Time to eat / written and illustrated by Steve Jenkins and Robin Page.
      p. cm.
   ISBN 978-0-547-25032-8
   1. Animals—Food—Juvenile literature. I. Page, Robin, 1957– II. Title.
   QL756.5.J46 2011
      591.5'3—dc22
2010025127

Manufactured in Mexico
RDT 10 9 8 7 6 5 4 3 2
4500351095